PAUL ROMAN

HOCKEY
SUPERSTARS
2024-2025

Your complete guide to the 2024–2025 season,
featuring action photos of
your favorite players

SCHOLASTIC

TORONTO NEW YORK LONDON AUCKLAND SYDNEY
MEXICO CITY NEW DELHI HONG KONG BUENOS AIRES

THE TEAMS

CALGARY FLAMES
team colors: red, gold, black and white
home arena: Scotiabank Saddledome
mascot: Harvey the Hound
Stanley Cups won: 1

EDMONTON OILERS
team colors: white, royal blue and orange
home arena: Rogers Place
mascot: Hunter
Stanley Cups won: 5

ANAHEIM DUCKS
team colors: black, gold, orange and silver
home arena: Honda Center
mascot: Wild Wing
Stanley Cups won: 1

LOS ANGELES KINGS
team colors: white, black and silver
home arena: Crypto.com Arena
mascot: Bailey
Stanley Cups won: 2

SEATTLE KRAKEN
team colors: dark blue, medium blue, light blue and red
home arena: Climate Pledge Arena
mascot: Buoy

VANCOUVER CANUCKS
team colors: blue, silver, green and white
home arena: Rogers Arena
mascot: Fin

SAN JOSE SHARKS
team colors: teal, black, orange and white
home arena: SAP Center at San Jose
mascot: S.J. Sharkie

VEGAS GOLDEN KNIGHTS
team colors: steel gray, gold, red and black
home arena: T-Mobile Arena
mascot: Chance
Stanley Cups won: 1

CHICAGO BLACKHAWKS
nickname: Hawks
team colors: red, black and white
home arena: United Center
mascot: Tommy Hawk
Stanley Cups won: 6

COLORADO AVALANCHE
nickname: Avs
team colors: burgundy, silver, black, blue and white
home arena: Ball Arena
mascot: Bernie
Stanley Cups won: 3

DALLAS STARS
team colors: green, white, black and silver
home arena: American Airlines Center
mascot: Victor E. Green
Stanley Cups won: 1

NASHVILLE PREDATORS
nickname: Preds
team colors: dark blue, white and gold
home arena: Bridgestone Arena
mascot: Gnash

UTAH HOCKEY CLUB
team colors: black, white and light blue
home arena: Delta Center

MINNESOTA WILD
team colors: red, green, gold, wheat and white
home arena: Xcel Energy Center
mascot: Nordy

WINNIPEG JETS
team colors: dark blue, blue, gray, silver, red and white
home arena: Canada Life Centre
mascot: Mick E. Moose

ST. LOUIS BLUES
team colors: blue, gold, dark blue and white
home arena: Enterprise Center
mascot: Louie
Stanley Cups won: 1

EASTERN CONFERENCE – ATLANTIC DIVISION

TORONTO MAPLE LEAFS
nickname: Leafs
team colors: blue and white
home arena: Scotiabank Arena
mascot: Carlton the Bear
Stanley Cups won: 11

BUFFALO SABRES
team colors: royal blue, gold and white
home arena: KeyBank Center
mascot: Sabretooth

FLORIDA PANTHERS
nickname: Cats
team colors: red, navy blue and gold
home arena: Amerant Bank Arena
mascots: Stanley C. Panther and Viktor E. Ratt
Stanley Cups won: 1

OTTAWA SENATORS
nickname: Sens
team colors: black, red, gold and white
home arena: Canadian Tire Centre
mascot: Spartacat

TAMPA BAY LIGHTNING
nickname: Bolts
team colors: blue, black and white
home arena: Amalie Arena
mascot: ThunderBug
Stanley Cups won: 3

MONTREAL CANADIENS
nickname: Habs
team colors: red, blue and white
home arena: Bell Centre
mascot: Youppi!
Stanley Cups won: 24

DETROIT RED WINGS
nickname: Wings
team colors: red and white
home arena: Little Caesars Arena
mascot (unofficial): Al the Octopus
Stanley Cups won: 11

BOSTON BRUINS
nickname: Bs
team colors: gold, black and white
home arena: TD Garden
mascot: Blades
Stanley Cups won: 6

EASTERN CONFERENCE – METROPOLITAN DIVISION

NEW YORK RANGERS
nickname: Blueshirts
team colors: blue, white and red
home arena: Madison Square Garden
Stanley Cups won: 4

COLUMBUS BLUE JACKETS
nickname: Jackets
team colors: blue, red and silver
home arena: Nationwide Arena
mascot: Stinger

WASHINGTON CAPITALS
nickname: Caps
team colors: red, navy blue and white
home arena: Capital One Arena
mascot: Slapshot
Stanley Cups won: 1

NEW YORK ISLANDERS
nickname: Isles
team colors: orange, blue and white
home arena: UBS Arena
mascot: Sparky the Dragon
Stanley Cups won: 4

PITTSBURGH PENGUINS
nickname: Pens
team colors: black, gold and white
home arena: PPG Paints Arena
mascot: Iceburgh
Stanley Cups won: 5

PHILADELPHIA FLYERS
team colors: orange, white and black
home arena: Wells Fargo Center
mascot: Gritty
Stanley Cups won: 2

NEW JERSEY DEVILS
team colors: red, black and white
home arena: Prudential Center
mascot: N.J. Devil
Stanley Cups won: 3

CAROLINA HURRICANES
nickname: Canes
team colors: red, black, gray and white
home arena: PNC Arena
mascots: Stormy and Caroline
Stanley Cups won: 1

YOUR FAVORITE TEAM

Name of your favorite team: _____

Conference and division: _____

Players on your favorite team at the start of the season:

Number	Name	Position
_____	_____	_____
_____	_____	_____
_____	_____	_____
_____	_____	_____
_____	_____	_____
_____	_____	_____
_____	_____	_____
_____	_____	_____
_____	_____	_____
_____	_____	_____
_____	_____	_____
_____	_____	_____
_____	_____	_____
_____	_____	_____

Changes, Trades, New Players

_____   _____   _____
_____   _____   _____
_____   _____   _____
_____   _____   _____
_____   _____   _____
_____   _____   _____
_____   _____   _____

End-of-Season Standings

Fill in the name of the team you think will finish in first place in each of the four NHL divisions.

WESTERN CONFERENCE

_____   **PACIFIC DIVISION**

_____   **CENTRAL DIVISION**

EASTERN CONFERENCE

ATLANTIC DIVISION   _____

METROPOLITAN DIVISION   _____

The Playoffs

Which two teams will meet in the Stanley Cup Final? Fill in their names below, then circle the team you think will win.

Eastern Conference Winner: _____

Western Conference Winner: _____

YOUR FAVORITE TEAM

Your Team — All Season Long

The standings of hockey teams are listed at NHL.com and on the sports pages of the newspaper all season long. The standings will show you which team is in first place, second place, etc., right down to last place.

Some of the abbreviations you'll become familiar with are: GP for games played; W for wins; L for losses; OT for overtime losses; PTS for points; A for assists; G for goals.

Check the standings on the same day of every month and copy down what they say about your team. By keeping track of your team this way you'll be able to see when it was playing well and when it wasn't.

	GP	W	L	OT	PTS
NOVEMBER 1					
DECEMBER 1					
JANUARY 1					
FEBRUARY 1					
MARCH 1					
APRIL 1					
MAY 1					

Final Standings

At the end of the season print the final record of your team below.

YOUR TEAM	GP	W	L	OT	PTS

Your Favorite Players' Scoring Records

While you're keeping track of your favorite team during the season, you can also follow the progress of your favorite players. Just fill in their point totals on the same day of every month.

player	nov 1	dec 1	jan 1	feb 1	mar 1	apr 1	may 1

Your Favorite Goaltenders' Records

You can keep track of your favorite goaltenders' averages during the season. Just fill in the information below.

GAA is the abbreviation for goals-against average. That's the average number of goals given up by a goaltender during a game over the course of the season.

goaltender	nov 1	dec 1	jan 1	feb 1	mar 1	apr 1	may 1

CONNOR BEDARD

Connor Bedard's first season in the NHL was exactly what you would have expected from a first overall draft pick: He led all rookies in scoring (22-39-61) and won the Calder Trophy. But there was also some of the unexpected in the 18-year-old's first NHL season. In a game against the New Jersey Devils on January 5, as he carried the puck in over the Devils' blueline on a power play, Connor dropped his glance for just a heartbeat. But it was long enough that he didn't see Devils defenseman Brendan Smith. Shoulder met jaw, and Connor found himself out of the lineup with a broken jaw for the next six weeks. It wasn't something he was expecting to have to go through that early in his career.

"I want to play games," said Connor. "I mean, it's frustrating watching and you can't be out there with your guys and try to help them win and go to battle with them."

As for highlight reel goals, there were many, but the goal that had everyone talking was a "Michigan-style" goal — where the puck is scooped onto the blade of the stick, lacrosse style, and fired into the net — against the St. Louis Blues on December 23. Connor was behind the Blues' goal when he scooped up the puck and darted out from behind the net to the left of goaltender Jordan Binnington. He lifted his stick, with the puck on the blade, and stuffed it, shoulder height, in behind a surprised Binnington.

> "We're all just trying to be ourselves, and I get a lot of inspiration from everyone in this room. Coming in as a young kid, not really knowing anyone, I've been really comfortable the whole time."

"I couldn't do what he did tonight," said none other than a man many consider to be the greatest player ever, Wayne Gretzky, who was at the game. "My daughter Emma is with me and she goes, 'Dad, did you ever do that?' I said, 'No, I could never do that.'"

By the time Connor Bedard calls it a career, you can expect that there will be many players, past and present, who will be saying exactly the same thing.

DID YOU KNOW?

Connor holds the Canadian National Junior Team record for most points in a single tournament. At the 2023 World Junior Hockey Championship he racked up 23 points, helping Canada to a gold medal.

HOCKEY MEMORIES

Connor grew up in North Vancouver, where winters aren't cold enough for backyard rinks. So he made do in the house, on roller blades with a stick and a ball. "Stick-handling, shooting and imagining game 7, Stanley Cup Finals kinda stuff, like any kid, and that's when I fell in love with it."

2023–2024 STATS

GP	G	A	PTS
68	22	39	61

Chicago Blackhawks' 1st choice, 1st overall, in 2023 NHL Entry Draft
1st NHL Team, season: Chicago Blackhawks, 2023–2024
Born: July 17, 2005 in North Vancouver, British Columbia
Plays: Center
Shoots: Right
Height: 1.78 m (5'10")
Weight: 84 kg (185 lbs.)

COLE CAUFIELD

What jumps out when you look at stats from Cole Caufield's hockey career? Goals. He can score. In high school he scored 82 goals in 50 games. With the U.S. National Team Development Program he scored 126 goals over two seasons. With the University of Wisconsin, he scored 30 goals in 31 games. As an NHL rookie he scored 23 goals, and he followed up with 26 the next season. So last season, Montreal fans thought Cole would take a run at the 30- or maybe even 40-goal mark. That didn't happen. While he finished with a respectable 28 goals, when you're playing for a legendary franchise, people ask questions: Has he lost his touch? Maybe he doesn't have the size to score consistently in the NHL? But Cole was just working hard to make sure his game was more well-rounded. He wanted to be able to set up goals as well as he could score them.

"I just wanted to score. I thought if I wasn't scoring, I probably wasn't doing much else," said Cole. "But now, if I'm not scoring, I still feel like I'm effective out there creating things."

The numbers back that up. He finished last season with a career-high 37 assists, more than his previous two seasons combined.

"I think he's seeing the ice better than when he came into the league," says Montreal captain Nick Suzuki. "He's a dual-threat player and it makes him harder to defend."

"The pressure and the love that the fans have for the team — they just want your team to succeed. I don't think there's any fanbase that really thinks about the team as much as Montreal does. It's a pleasure to play here. It's just a great spot to play hockey."

Suzuki and Caufield, along with head coach Marty St. Louis, believe they have what it takes to get Montreal back into the top tier of NHL teams.

"I think that the culture we have and the positivity learning about the game that we have, it's kind of contagious around the room," says Cole. "Everybody who is part of the organization these days is headed in the right direction."

DID YOU KNOW?
Cole's dad, Paul, is the all-time leading scorer at the University of Wisconsin-Stevens Point, and his grandfather, Wayne, was a longtime pro in the Eastern Hockey League and the U.S. Hockey League.

HOCKEY MEMORIES
Cole's mom, Kelly, remembers Cole crying his eyes out when he was two years old because he wanted to be out on skates like his older brother Brock. He got his chance after Brock had moved up a group. "Cole was out there with his diaper on, but he loved every second of it."

2023–2024 STATS

GP	G	A	PTS
82	28	37	65

Montreal Canadiens' 1st choice, 15th overall, in 2019 NHL Entry Draft
1st NHL Team, season: Montreal Canadiens, 2021–2022
Born: January 2, 2001, in Mosinee, Wisconsin
Plays: Right Wing
Shoots: Right
Height: 1.73 m (5'8")
Weight: 79.5 kg (175 lbs.)

BLAKE COLEMAN

CALGARY FLAMES

Over 1300 players have had their names engraved on the Stanley Cup, but only one of those players was born and raised in Texas, and his name is on the Cup twice — Calgary Flames forward Blake Coleman. Blake was a big part of the Tampa Bay Lightning's back-to-back Cups in 2020 and 2021. After the second Cup, the Lightning had to make some salary cap decisions and Blake became an unrestricted free agent, signing a six-year deal with the Calgary Flames. It can be a roll of the dice when a team signs a player as a free agent, but you'd have to say that the Calgary Flames made the right call. In three seasons with the Flames, Blake has reeled off two of the highest point totals of his career, including last season's career best 54 points (30 goals, 24 assists). Despite his touch around the net, Blake doesn't see himself as a classic NHL sniper.

"I don't typically score the highlight reel goals," he says. "I've been able to score at every level that I've played, but they've always just kind of been workmanlike goals." Some fans may beg to differ; he has definitely scored a few beautiful goals in his career.

> "My game is based around compete and forechecking and smarts in the game. I don't want to change much. I'm not going to be making backhand, toe-drag plays or anything like that."

"They called me 'The Human Zamboni' when I was a kid playing hockey," Blake says with a smile. "For whatever reason, I'd always end up on my stomach after a goal."

Some may refer to that as "having style" — something Blake has loads of when he's off the ice as well. It's not unusual to see him wearing a classic cowboy hat when he arrives for games. The Stetson was a birthday gift from his wife last season.

"It's a little out there, but it's fun to mix it up a little bit," he says.

Makes perfect sense. The man from Plano, Texas, wearing a cowboy hat. If he can work some playoff magic with the Flames in the next few seasons he could have himself a hat trick of Stanley Cups.

DID YOU KNOW?

Blake's wife, Jordan, performed in front of bigger crowds than Blake ever has. She was a cheerleader for the NFL's Dallas Cowboys, who regularly play home games in front of crowds of 80,000 or more.

HOCKEY MEMORIES

"My grandma took me to Dallas Stars games. She was from New York, so she got season tickets. She took me because nobody wanted to go, because they didn't know what hockey was. I started going when I was two and started playing when I was four."

GP	G	A	PTS
78	30	24	54

New Jersey Devils' 2nd choice, 75th overall, in 2011 NHL Entry Draft
1st NHL Team, season: New Jersey Devils, 2016–2017
Born: November 28, 1991 in Plano, Texas, USA
Plays: Center
Shoots: Left
Height: 1.80 m (5'11")
Weight: 90.5 kg (199 lbs.)

THATCHER DEMKO

It's safe to say that there's never been a more successful NHL goalie from San Diego, California, than Thatcher Demko. That's where he grew up and first fell in love with the game of hockey and the position of goaltender.

> *"For me, it's just trying to put a smile on your face. I know it sounds stupid, but there's stuff that goes on in the brain when you physically smile. It changes your mindset a bit, reminds you that everything is going to be okay and the sun is coming up tomorrow."*

Thatcher's career started to capture attention during his 2013–2014 season with the Boston College Eagles in the NCAA. As a freshman, he went 16-5-3 with a save percentage of .919 and a goals-against average of 2.24. NHL scouts took note and Thatcher soon found himself as the top-ranked goalie in the 2014 NHL Entry Draft. The Vancouver Canucks snagged him in the second round. After finishing his college career and developing his game in the minors for a few seasons, Thatcher found himself in Vancouver with the big club. By the 2020–2021 season, he was the team's number-one goalie and feeling all of the pressure that goes with playing that role in a city like Vancouver.

"I'm from San Diego. I didn't even know what *Hockey Night in Canada* was until I got drafted and turned pro," says Thatcher. "Everyone tells you the Canadian market is tough, but you don't really know that until you're experiencing it."

Thatcher has responded to the pressure in a big way, developing into one of the best goalies in the NHL and playing his part in making the Canucks one of the best teams in the league.

Unfortunately, injuries caught up to Thatcher during last year's Vancouver playoff run and he wasn't able to play in the Western Conference Final against Edmonton. There are fewer things tougher on players than not being able to play in a big game. There is no doubt that missing last year's playoffs will provide lots of inspiration for Thatcher this season.

DID YOU KNOW?

Thatcher made his NHL debut on March 31, 2018, when he was called up for a single game. He backstopped the Canucks to a 5-4 overtime win. He spent most of the next season in the minors before sticking with the Canucks the next season.

HOCKEY MEMORIES

"I was always drawn to playing goalie. Sometimes when you're a kid you switch around positions, but I think I was around 10 years old when I stuck with it full time."

2023–2024 STATS

GP	W	L	OT	GAA	SO
51	35	14	2	2.45	5

Vancouver Canucks' 3rd choice, 36th overall, in 2014 NHL Entry Draft
1st NHL Team, season: Vancouver Canucks, 2017–2018
Born: December 8, 1995, in San Diego, California
Plays: Goaltender
Catches: Left
Height: 1.93 m (6'4")
Weight: 87 kg (192 lbs.)

CONNOR HELLEBUYCK

There was a time when it was common for an NHL player to spend his entire career with the same team. There was no players' association, there were fewer teams and there was no such thing as a free agent. In today's NHL, in simple terms, a player who has been in the league for seven seasons, or is over the age of 27, is free to sign with any team that makes him an offer he's happy with. Players have different priorities and needs, but it's safe to say that every player who pulls on an NHL sweater wants to play on a team that has a chance to win the Stanley Cup.

Heading into last season, Winnipeg superstar goalie Connor Hellebuyck was one season away from becoming an unrestricted free agent. He had some big decisions to make. Were the Jets going to continue to be competitive? Did the team believe he was the guy who could lead them to a championship? Connor was convinced that the answer to both of those questions was yes, and, in October of 2023, he signed a seven-year contract with the Jets.

"I think that this organization believes in me the way I believe in myself," reflected Connor at a press conference after he'd signed the deal. "That breeds success . . . Now I'm ready to be a Jet for life and bring a Cup to this city because I truly believe that we can get it done here."

For his part, Connor continued to get it done for the Jets. He was awarded the Vezina Trophy as the NHL's top goalie, finishing with 37 wins and a .921 save percentage.

> "A lot of times I'll know where the puck is going before the guy even shoots based on where guys are on the ice, what's open and what did I give? It's more experience than anything."

As Connor heads into his 10th season with the Jets it seems more and more as though he was destined to spend his entire career with the team. No doubt the Jets figure they're getting their money's worth from a player who believes in them as much as they believe in him.

DID YOU KNOW?

Connor already tops the franchise list in wins, save percentage and shutouts; he's also the only goalie in franchise history to have won the Vezina Trophy.

HOCKEY MEMORIES

Even as a kid playing road hockey, Connor drifted towards playing goal. However, he does remember being a road hockey goalie could be a bit of a painful experience: "In road hockey you have a chest pad, but I'd take shots off the arm all the time and it really killed!"

2023–2024 STATS

GP	W	L	OT	GAA	SO
60	37	19	4	2.39	5

Winnipeg Jets' 4th choice, 130th overall, in 2012 NHL Entry Draft
1st NHL Team, season: Winnipeg Jets, 2015–2016
Born: May 19, 1993, in Commerce, Michigan
Plays: Goaltender
Catches: Left
Height: 1.93 m (6'4")
Weight: 94 kg (207 lbs.)

ROOPE HINTZ

Perseverance means sticking with something, continuing to work towards a goal even when it's difficult or takes longer than you would like. Roope Hintz needed loads a few seasons back, when a persistent injury forced him to play most of the games feeling less than 100 percent. It all went back to game four of the 2020 Stanley Cup Final against the Tampa Bay Lightning. Early in the second period an opponent's stick got caught up in Roope's skates. He toppled into the boards and eventually limped his way to the dressing room. He never returned to the series.

"I don't know if it was from the hit . . ." recalled Roope. "But when I stepped on the stick, something happened there."

Roope rested in the off-season. But at training camp, the groin injury resurfaced. It was determined that, although it would be uncomfortable, Roope could play with no risk of making it worse, so he decided to help his team out during the pandemic-shortened season. He finally had surgery after season's end.

"I found a way to manage it," said Roope. "[I'd] been playing well, so why not play and help the team win?"

> "He's developed into one of our most versatile players, making an impact on special teams and at even strength, and can be counted on by our coaching staff in every situation."
> — Dallas general manager Jim Nill

That perseverance paid off for Roope in a few ways. The Dallas section of the Professional Hockey Writer's Association nominated him for the Bill Masterton Trophy, awarded for "perseverance, sportsmanship and dedication." Despite the pain, he had a solid season, finishing with 43 points in 41 games. And his hard work was rewarded with an eight-year contract extension in November of 2022. Since then he has been one of the best players on the Stars. That includes an incredible run during the 2023 playoffs where he picked up 24 points (10 goals, 14 assists) in 19 games.

"He's a big powerful man that won't get intimidated, won't get pushed out of any game," said Dallas coach Peter DeBoer.

That's what you need to be an NHL superstar.

DID YOU KNOW?

Roope's nickname is "Ace of Spades." It comes from a tattoo on his left forearm of three playing cards, one of which is the ace of spades.

HOCKEY MEMORIES

As a kid, Roope played many different sports — soccer, basketball and a Finnish version of baseball called Pesäpallo — but he decided to focus on hockey. "I was my best at hockey and I like it the most. Plus, it was what my older brother did, so it made an easy decision."

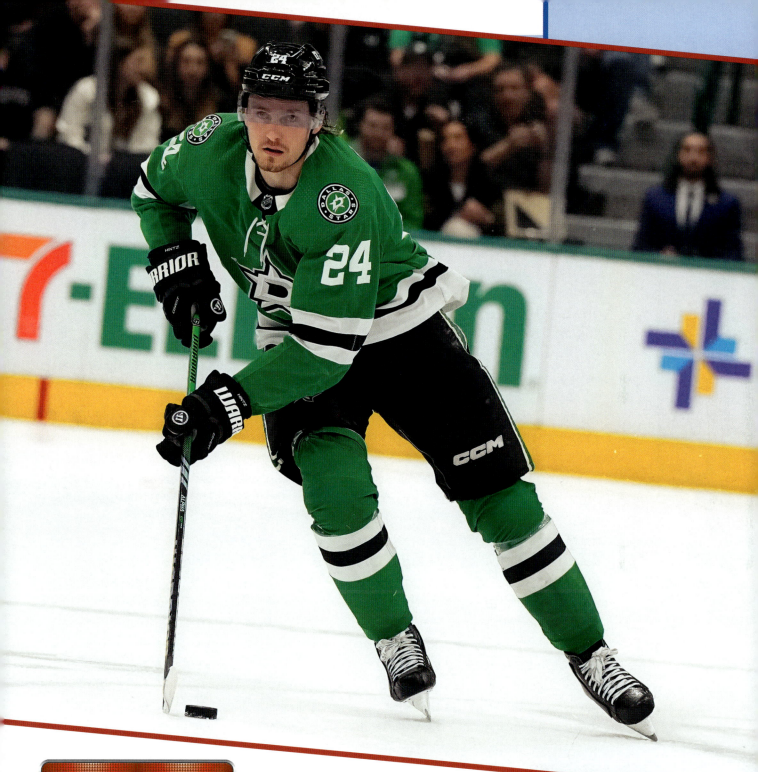

GP	G	A	PTS
80	30	35	65

Dallas Stars' 2nd choice, 49th overall, in 2015 NHL Entry Draft
1st NHL Team, season: Dallas Stars, 2018–2019
Born: November 17, 1996, in Nokia, Finland
Plays: Center
Shoots: Left
Height: 1.90 m (6'3")
Weight: 96 kg (212 lbs.)

Quinn Hughes

A couple of seasons back, in his fourth season with the Vancouver Canucks, Quinn Hughes let it be known that he was feeling that the time was right for him to step into more of a leadership role.

"I think I've always been a good leader," he said at the time. "I don't feel I need to change who I am, but if it's also taking a more vocal role on the team, then I feel comfortable doing that."

Vancouver management clearly felt the same way. Quinn was named the 15th captain in team history prior to the start of last season.

"Quinn is very well-liked and respected inside our dressing room," said Vancouver general manager Patrik Allvin at the time of the announcement. "We know that he'll continue to grow and develop in his leadership skills in the years to come."

Some captains like to be vocal, and others prefer to lead by example. Quinn does a bit of both. He will voice an opinion in the dressing room when it is called for, but he also leads with his play on the ice. There was a game, at home late last season against Buffalo, when he felt his team needed a boost. He happened to catch Buffalo forward Victor Olofsson cutting across the Canucks' blueline with the puck. The next thing Olofsson knew, he was on the ice after being crushed by a big open-ice hit from Quinn. The crowd roared its approval.

> "There are a lot of ways to lead, and Quinn does it by example and by always giving his teammates, coaches and the organization the utmost respect."
> — Vancouver head coach Rick Tocchet

"It was almost like I'd scored a goal," said Quinn.

That tipped the momentum in the Canucks' favour and they went on to win the game.

Quinn is coming off the best season of his career. He led all NHL defensemen in scoring with 92 points (17 goals, 75 assists) and was named the Norris Trophy winner. It's clear why there was really only one choice when it came to the Canucks picking a new captain.

DID YOU KNOW?

Quinn hit the 40-point mark faster than any other defenseman last season. He picked up the 40th in his 31st game of the season. No other Canucks defenseman had ever scored 40 points in fewer than 40 games.

HOCKEY MEMORIES

Quinn began in minor hockey as a forward. A coach advised him to switch to defense when he was around 12 years old. "I just remember my Dad asking me, 'Are you sure you want to play D?' and I said 'Yeah, I want to play D.' And that was the end of the conversation."

2023–2024 STATS

GP	G	A	PTS
82	17	75	92

Vancouver Canucks' 1st choice, 7th overall, in 2018 NHL Entry Draft
1st NHL Team, season: Vancouver Canucks, 2019–2020
Born: October 14, 1999, in Orlando, Florida
Plays: Defense
Shoots: Left
Height: 1.78 m (5'10")
Weight: 82 kg (180 lbs.)

COLORADO AVALANCHE

Heading into the 2024–2025 season, Nathan MacKinnon is playing the best hockey of his career. Last season he set a career mark of 140 points and won both the Hart Trophy as NHL MVP and the Ted Lindsay Award, the MVP award voted on by fellow players. Nathan just keeps getting better and better.

"Once he reaches the bar, he's going to raise the bar again and try to push towards it again," says Colorado head coach Jared Bednar. "That's the competitor in him. That's the perfectionist in him. All he thinks about is winning."

And win he has. Nathan won the Calder Trophy as the NHL's best rookie in 2014 and the Lady Byng Trophy as the NHL's Most Gentlemanly Player in 2020. There was a Memorial Cup Championship in 2013 with Halifax, a World Championship with Canada in 2015 and, the ultimate, a Stanley Cup Championship with Colorado in 2022. With that last big goal accomplished, you'd wonder if Nathan might back off a little in terms of his intensity and drive. But those who watch him every day will tell you that, if anything, he's gotten even more intense and determined to win.

Last season he put up the longest consecutive points scoring streak of his career (November 20, 2023 through December 27, 2023: 19 games, 36 points) as well as becoming the only player in Avalanche history to record back-to-back 100-point seasons. Those are hardly signs of a player backing off on the intensity level.

> "Some of my favorite players ever have won this trophy [the Hart] . . . So, super happy and excited to share it with my teammates. It's a team award. You need great players around you."

"If anything maybe I'm a little wiser now," says Nathan. "The passion has been there my entire life. I don't think it's going anywhere. I learned a lot from that Cup run [in 2022] and I learned a lot from the failures before that and I'm trying to shape myself into the best leader I can be for the team."

After another great season, the bar has been pushed even higher. Here's betting that Nathan, once again, meets the challenge.

DID YOU KNOW?
In 2014, Nathan was the youngest player in NHL history to win the Calder Trophy as the league's top rookie, at the age of 18 years, 224 days.

HOCKEY MEMORIES
Nathan's childhood home was next to a small lake that would freeze over in the winter. Nathan spent hours and hours skating on the rink and firing pucks with friends and, sometimes, by himself. "I just remember never not wanting to go to the rink. I always loved to play."

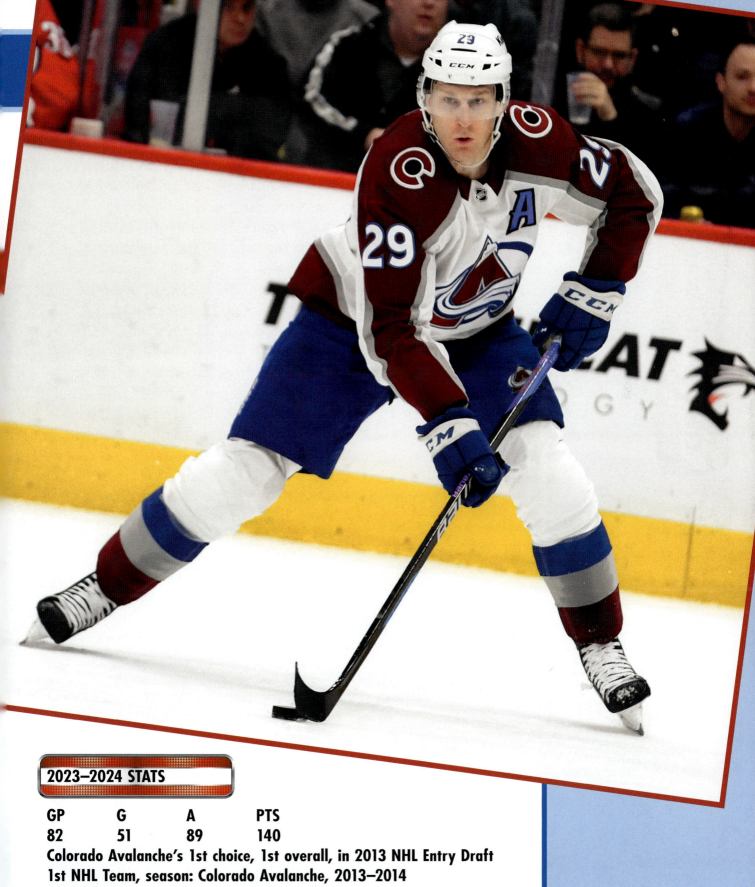

2023–2024 STATS

GP	G	A	PTS
82	51	89	140

Colorado Avalanche's 1st choice, 1st overall, in 2013 NHL Entry Draft
1st NHL Team, season: Colorado Avalanche, 2013–2014
Born: September 1, 1995, in Halifax, Nova Scotia
Plays: Center
Shoots: Right
Height: 1.83 m (6'0")
Weight: 91 kg (200 lbs.)

CALE MAKAR

Ask a fan what impresses them the most about Cale Makar's game and you'll get several different answers: his poise and maturity on the ice; his great puck handling skills; his on-ice vision. But the aspect that would be mentioned the most would be Cale's fantastic skating ability. He isn't the fastest straight-line skater in the league — that would be Connor McDavid — but Cale has an amazing ability to change direction and accelerate very quickly in tight spaces. The players refer to it as having "good edges."

"I don't think anyone in the world has the same potential as Makar. That's just reality."
— Dallas Stars' coach Pete DeBoer

"My skating has always been a work-in-progress," says Cale. "I'm always trying to learn new things. I think, from a young age, there was a lot of repetition and drills. Also, I always loved playing forward at a young age. That gives you a great opportunity to work on your skating as well. Then, I started loving it at the back end [playing defense], then you figure out how to skate backwards and just keep working on it."

So far, Cale's career has blown along with the force of a hurricane. His NHL debut came in the Stanley Cup playoffs in 2019, and he scored the game-winning goal in his first game. In 2020, he won the Calder Trophy as the NHL's top rookie. In 2022, the Avalanche won the Stanley Cup Championship and Cale took home the Conn Smythe Trophy as playoff MVP and the Norris Trophy as the NHL's best defenseman. He's coming off a career-high 90 points. At 23 years old, after only three full seasons, he's accomplished more than most players do in an entire career. But Cale never dwells on that.

"My dad always gives me the 'one day you'll look back and remember all of this,'" says Cale. "But, for me, right now, I just try to stay in the moment and not get all caught up in the individual stuff."

There's something to add to the list of Cale's great attributes as a hockey player: "keeping things in perspective."

DID YOU KNOW?
Along with Cale, only two other defensemen in the history of the NHL have their name on the Stanley Cup, the Calder Trophy, the Conn Smythe Trophy and the Norris Trophy: Hall of Famers Bobby Orr and Brian Leetch.

HOCKEY MEMORIES
Cale was drafted out of the Alberta Junior Hockey League, playing for the Brooks Bandits. "I feel like there are so many little habits that I learned with that team . . . the amount of things I learned there were incredible and play so many roles in my game nowadays."

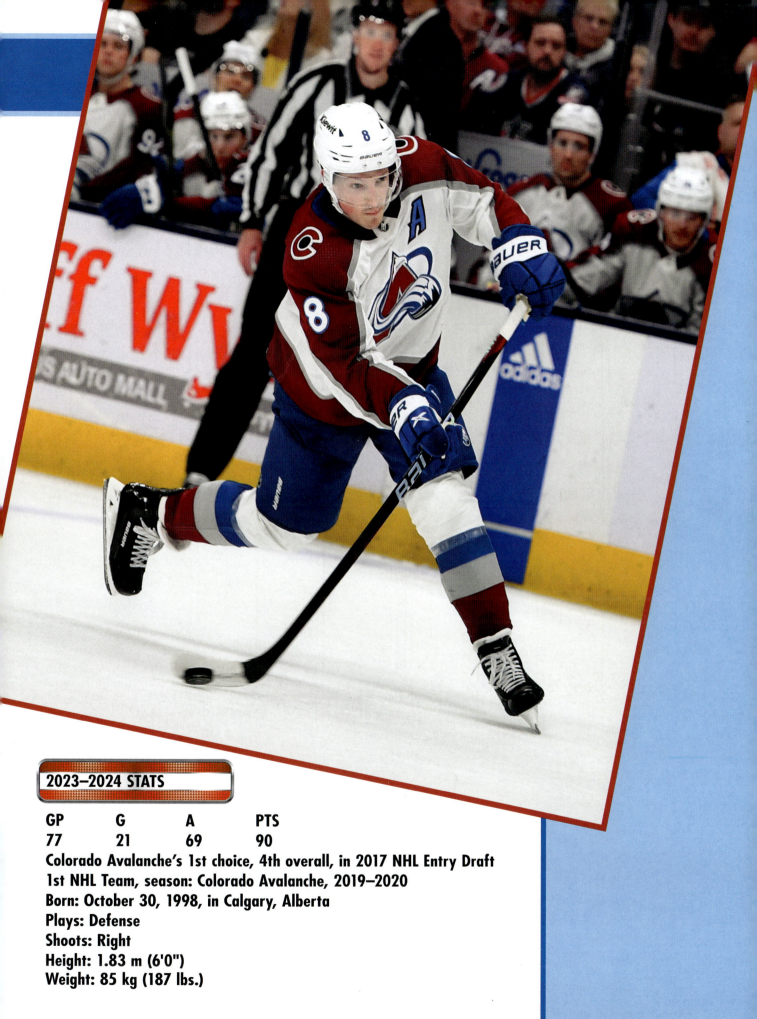

GP	G	A	PTS
77	21	69	90

Colorado Avalanche's 1st choice, 4th overall, in 2017 NHL Entry Draft
1st NHL Team, season: Colorado Avalanche, 2019–2020
Born: October 30, 1998, in Calgary, Alberta
Plays: Defense
Shoots: Right
Height: 1.83 m (6'0")
Weight: 85 kg (187 lbs.)

AUSTON MATTHEWS

TORONTO MAPLE LEAFS

There were times last season when Auston Matthews made scoring goals look so easy that even his teammates had to remind themselves of how tough it actually is to score in the best hockey league in the world.

"You're going to have ups and downs. I think it's just making sure you work that much harder and push through it . . . making sure you can make an impact in whatever way possible."

"You're sitting on the bench, leaning over, looking at teammates and saying, 'That was crazy,' said Bobby McMann after a Matthews hat trick performance last season. "You have to recognize how amazing it is, and you just love having him on your team."

Auston won the Maurice Richard Trophy as the league's top goal scorer for the third time in the last four seasons, finishing up with 69 goals and breaking his own club record of 60, set in 2021–2022.

Picking Auston's best games of last season is no easy task, but here are a couple to consider: February 17, 2024 in Anaheim, Auston scored early in the first period to put the Leafs on top. He added an assist in the first before picking up two goals and an assist in the second for a career-best five points in two periods! Four nights later, in Tempe, Arizona, against the Coyotes, Matthews rattled off a pair of goals to surpass the 50-goal mark for the second time in his career. Making that night extra special was the fact that Auston was raised in nearby Scottsdale, and the stands were packed with dozens of good friends and family.

"He was in his hometown. A lot of people here, a lot of family, a lot of loved ones," said teammate Mitch Marner after the game. "He's meant a lot to this city. So, to get his 50th goal here, it was pretty special."

A special night, during another special season, for the man who continues to make it look easy — even though we know it's not.

DID YOU KNOW?
Auston is pals with pop star Justin Bieber. They met at a home game in 2019 and have become fast friends. "He's so talented," says Auston about Bieber. "The work and preparation that he puts into his craft is actually very inspiring for me."

HOCKEY MEMORIES
Auston clearly remembers falling in love with the sport when he saw his first Coyotes game. "My uncle had season tickets, so that's how I got into hockey. I definitely had a passion for it when I started playing hockey."

2023–2024 STATS

GP	G	A	PTS
81	69	38	107

Toronto Maple Leafs' 1st choice, 1st overall, in 2016 NHL Entry Draft
1st NHL Team, season: Toronto Maple Leafs, 2016–2017
Born: September 17, 1997, in San Ramon, California
Plays: Center
Shoots: Left
Height: 1.90 m (6'3")
Weight: 97.5 kg (215 lbs.)

CONNOR McDAVID

EDMONTON OILERS

It was classic Connor McDavid: The Edmonton Oilers trailed the Florida Panthers three games to none in last year's Stanley Cup Final. After battling to turn around their season and then push all the way through to the Final, the thought of crashing out in four straight games wasn't a good one. Connor dug in and led the Oilers through the next two games, picking up a goal and three assists in Game Four and another two goals and two assists in Game Five. The Oilers were back in the series and forced it to a seventh and deciding game where they ultimately fell short, losing to the Panthers 2–1.

> "He's the greatest player ever to play, in my books. There are so many things that people don't see that he does. He single-handedly turned our franchise around, pretty much. I just love sharing the ice with him and he's a really, really special person."
> —teammate Leon Draisaitl

Still, the numbers spoke of an amazing playoff performance. He led all post-season scorers with 42 points in 25 games. Only Wayne Gretzky and Mario Lemieux have scored more points in a single post-season. Connor was named the winner of the Conn Smythe Trophy as the playoff MVP, only the sixth time a player on the losing team had won it.

As Connor heads into his 10th NHL season, it's worth taking a look at just a few of the many amazing things he's managed to accomplish so far in his career: five-time winner of the Art Ross Trophy as the NHL's leading scorer, one of only six players in NHL history to win the award five or more times. Three-time winner of the Hart Trophy as the NHL MVP and four-time winner of the Ted Lindsay Award, given to the league's best player in a vote from fellow players. Sixth-fastest player to hit the 600 career-point mark. Fifth-fastest player in NHL history to record 900 career points.

All things being equal, Connor will register his 1000th career point early this season and he will be the fourth-fastest in league history to hit that mark.

DID YOU KNOW?

Away from the ice, Connor is a big fan of the band Nickelback and the TV series *Friends*. "My brother and I grew up watching *Friends*, like, every day. We had all of the seasons on DVD. As soon as we got to the end, we'd start again."

HOCKEY MEMORIES

Connor has hopes for a future memory: playing for Canada at the Olympic Games. "It would be a dream come true. To have an opportunity to play in a best-on-best tournament and represent my country, to play with other amazing hockey players from Canada, that would be special."

2023–2024 STATS

GP	G	A	PTS
76	32	100	132

Edmonton Oilers' 1st choice, 1st overall, in 2015 NHL Entry Draft
1st NHL Team, season: Edmonton Oilers, 2015–2016
Born: January 13, 1997, in Richmond Hill, Ontario
Plays: Center
Shoots: Left
Height: 1.85 m (6'1")
Weight: 88 kg (194 lbs.)

DARNELL NURSE

When the Edmonton Oilers took Darnell Nurse seventh overall in the 2013 NHL Draft there were those who wondered about the choice. Historically, the Oilers had been particularly cautious when it came to taking a defenseman with their first pick. But Darnell was special. The Edmonton general manager at the time, Craig MacTavish, said so.

> "There's no one that's gonna expect more out of me than me. That's something that has been instilled in me since I was very young."

"He's a guy that, over time — we'll have to be patient with him — is going to provide us with toughness. And he's the guy that will ride shotgun for a lot of our other first round picks, our skilled players, for many years."

While Darnell's size does make him an intimidating physical force on the ice, he has many other important roles. He plays a lot of minutes, averaging 21:53 per game last season. Most of those minutes come against the other team's top players. He also sees time on the penalty kill and power play. After Kris Knoblauch became coach last season, Darnell saw even more responsibility in key situations.

"He's such a good skater with a good stick, in close space," said Knoblauch. "We want him to be assertive, close that space and create turnovers."

For his part, heading into his 10th season with the Oilers, Darnell has grown to be one of the most respected and admired players, both on his team and in the league. His work ethic is second to none. Along with superstars like Connor McDavid and Leon Draisaitl, he helps set the tone on one of the NHL's best teams.

"To come in each and every day and make sure that when we're getting on the ice we're getting better," says Darnell. "We're not going to go out there and lollygag around and waste each other's time. Those two [McDavid and Draisaitl] are great examples of doing that from a very young age."

He's a leader and the Oilers best defenseman. As it turns out, taking Darnell in the first round all those years ago wasn't a gamble — it was a stroke of genius.

DID YOU KNOW?

In 2022, Darnell set up a scholarship at his former high school in Hamilton, Ontario. Two prizes are given out each year to students who have overcome adversity and need some financial help in order to continue their education.

HOCKEY MEMORIES

Darnell's childhood memories are of a very busy sports house! "When you talk about sacrifice — my parents had three kids who were playing high-end sports where they had to travel all around North America to go to tournaments. It all starts with them."

2023–2024 STATS

GP	G	A	PTS
81	10	22	32

Edmonton Oilers' 1st choice, 7th overall, in 2013 NHL Entry Draft
1st NHL Team, season: Edmonton Oilers, 2015–2016
Born: February 4, 1995, in Hamilton, Ontario
Plays: Defense
Shoots: Left
Height: 1.93 m (6'4")
Weight: 97.5 kg (215 lbs.)

DAVID PASTRNAK

BOSTON BRUINS

David Pastrnak can score goals at a pace that puts him alongside the best in the hockey world; there is absolutely no doubt about that. Since he started playing in the NHL in 2014–2015, he has scored more goals than Connor McDavid, Steven Stamkos and Sidney Crosby. Only two players have scored more goals over that period than the man they call "Pasta": Alex Ovechkin and Auston Matthews.

> "I want to get better every year, and that was my mojo since I got to the league, and I still have that."

"He's one of the best goal scorers in the game right now. Simple as that," said Pittsburgh coach Mike Sullivan after a game last season. "He's a threat 5-on-5, he's dangerous on the power play. He's one of the most dynamic offensive players in the league."

Aside from the goal scoring, last season Pasta also showed that he could be an even better playmaker than many gave him credit for. To go along with his 47 goals, he also added a career-high 63 assists.

"He's a great passer," said Colorado head coach Jared Bednar. "He uses his line mates well . . . He's a lot to handle. You have to be aware of a guy like him at all times."

Another thing David was determined to push to the next level was his role as a team leader. The Bruins were a team in transition last season. Veteran leaders like Patrice Bergeron, Zdeno Chara and David Krejci were all gone. It was time for other players to step into those roles. David wanted to make sure he was one of them.

"Those guys couldn't have prepared us any better," says David. "We were lucky and fortunate to be learning from them every single day. I'm ready to take that step and be a leader."

One of the ultimate ways to lead a team is to help lead that team to a championship. "I want to bring the championship back to Boston, and this has been my big motivation since I got into this room."

DID YOU KNOW?

Pasta loves his clothes! At last year's NHL All-Star Game in Toronto, he wore a custom-made outfit in Bruins colors: a bright yellow suit with a black shirt. "I'm just open minded, free. I wear what I want."

HOCKEY MEMORIES

One of David's closest friends in the game is Toronto's William Nylander. When David was 16 he moved to Sweden to play. "When we were together on the team and started playing together as a line it was like instant chemistry between us," recalls David.

2023–2024 STATS

GP	G	A	PTS
82	47	63	110

Boston Bruins' 1st choice, 25th overall, in 2014 NHL Entry Draft
1st NHL Team, season: Boston Bruins, 2014–2015
Born: May 25, 1996, in Havířov, Czechia
Plays: Right Wing
Shoots: Right
Height: 1.83 m (6'0")
Weight: 88.5 kg (195 lbs.)

JONATHAN QUICK

In the minds of many hockey fans, Jonathan will always be a Los Angeles King. The Kings drafted him, he played 15 seasons for them, and he was a big part of two Stanley Cups there (2012 and 2014). The Kings dealt him at the trade deadline in 2023 and he finished up that season in Las Vegas, where he was part of the Golden Knights' Stanley Cup Championship, although his role was limited to backing up Vegas' number-one goalie, Adin Hill. Jonathan signed as a free agent with the Rangers prior to last season. It was a homecoming of sorts, as the Rangers were the team Jonathan grew up watching.

> "I was very fortunate to be in one spot as long as I was. You take it [being traded] for what it is. You show up every day, you work hard and be a good teammate and try to help your team win games."

"I've been very fortunate to play with some great players over the course of my career," reflects Jonathan. "To end up here, with this organization and this group of guys, it's awesome."

A highlight for Jonathan last season came when he got to face the Kings.

He picked up a win against his old team in New York in December. Emotions must have been running high. How could they not, playing against a team that you spent the best years of your career with, only to have it end by being traded unexpectedly?

"Yeah, it's special, right?" said Jonathan after the game. "It was a long day . . . Having never played them before, the way it ended there, you're replaying a lot of the memories. There's a lot of thoughts running through your head. It was tough getting in the pre-game nap."

At this stage of his spectacular career, Jonathan mostly backs up the Rangers' number-one goalie, Igor Shesterkin. But that doesn't mean Jonathan isn't still busy racking up career milestones. Late last season he picked up career win number 392, making him the winningest American-born goalie in NHL history. He will undoubtedly tick the 400-career-wins box this season. He's a superstar, no matter what sweater he's wearing.

DID YOU KNOW?

On October 24, 2007, playing for the Reading Royals in the ECHL, Jonathan picked up his first professional win, his first professional shutout AND scored a goal as the Royals defeated the Pensacola Ice Pilots 3-0.

HOCKEY MEMORIES

"The street I grew up on, I grew up with a lot of kids my age and we all kind of got into hockey at the same time. After school we'd come home and play street hockey. We all played hockey. After a few years of playing defense, I talked my parents into letting me play goalie."

2023–2024 STATS

GP	W	L	OT	GAA	SO
27	18	6	2	2.62	2

Los Angeles Kings' 4th choice, 72nd overall, in 2005 NHL Entry Draft
1st NHL Team, season: L.A. Kings, 2008–2009
Born: January 21, 1986 in Milford, Connecticut
Plays: Goaltender
Catches: Left
Height: 1.85m (6'1")
Weight: 97.5 kg (215 lbs.)

SAM REINHART

Sam Reinhart was a high draft pick, and during six seasons with the Buffalo Sabres he was always among the top scorers on the team. After being traded to the Florida Panthers during the 2021 off-season he put up back-to-back 30-goal seasons and set a career high with 82 points. But last season Sam took the step from being a very good NHL player to being a superstar.

> "I think each year I've felt better and better. My first camp, my first time coming to Florida, the first thing I noticed was the depth. No matter where you're playing in the lineup, you're going to get some opportunity and you're going to be able to create."

One of the big improvements in Sam's game heading into last season was his speed. He worked hard during the off-season to get quicker and came to camp in elite condition. His better conditioning allowed him to go harder for longer.

"I probably feel a bit quicker than in years prior," said Sam early last season. "If I can gain a few more inches on the ice than I've had before, it's going to give me more time to make plays."

By late March Sam had hit a career high in points and, in a game against the Philadelphia Flyers on March 24, reached the 50-goal mark for the first time in his career.

"It's such a rare thing in a player's career," said Panthers' head coach Paul Maurice. "That puts you in an elite class . . . They're superstars."

Sam finished the season leading the team in scoring with a career-best 94 points (57 goals, 37 assists). He capped it all by scoring the game-winning goal in game seven of the Stanley Cup Final as the Panthers clinched the first championship in franchise history with a 2–1 win. It was a dream come true.

"You're hoping that's it [the go-ahead goal], right?" said Sam. "I mean, there was a lot of work still to do, a lot of game left, but absolutely I'm hoping that's the one."

DID YOU KNOW?

Sam is only the second player in the history of the Florida Panthers franchise to have a 50-goal season. The other was Pavel Bure, who managed the feat twice (in 1999–2000 and again in 2000–2001).

HOCKEY MEMORIES

Sam's father, Paul Reinhart, played 648 NHL games over 11 seasons in the '80s. "We learned so much from him. He was retired before we were born . . . but he still loved the game. I owe a lot about my passion and the way I think about the game to him."

2023–2024 STATS

GP	G	A	PTS
82	57	37	94

Buffalo Sabres' 1st choice, 2nd overall, in 2014 NHL Entry Draft
1st NHL Team, season: Buffalo Sabres, 2015–2016
Born: November 6, 1995, in West Vancouver, British Columbia
Plays: Center
Shoots: Right
Height: 1.88 m (6'2")
Weight: 87.5 kg (193 lbs.)

TIM STÜTZLE

Big things were predicted for Tim Stützle when he went third overall in the 2020 NHL Entry Draft. Ottawa scouts loved his size, his attitude and his touch around the net. Heading into his fifth season with the Sens, Tim is delivering on all fronts. He has led the Senators in scoring in each of the last two seasons and, so far, he has more career points (247) than any other player taken in the very highly regarded 2020 draft.

> "Everything is about having fun. Living life and enjoying every moment you get on the ice and in the room. We should appreciate everything we get and that we're able to play hockey."

"He's just such a special talent," says teammate Thomas Chabot. "The way he moves, the way he holds onto the puck. There is nobody else who can do it his way, which is what makes it so special."

Part of what makes Tim special, aside from the points, is how hard he has worked on other parts of his game: his play away from the puck, making sure he's always in the right position when he needs to be. His defensive play has improved so much that, on most nights, you'll find him on the top Ottawa penalty killing unit. Playing a two-way game is something that Ottawa coach Jacques Martin stresses to all of his players, but especially to his best players.

"Our young players, our core guys, they've got great skills," says Martin. "They've got to improve away from the puck. To me, it's more rewarding to win as a team."

"I think I've gotten better in my 200-foot game," adds Tim. "I think my best is when I'm playing a good offensive and defensive game."

Despite his best efforts, the young Ottawa superstar has yet to play in the Stanley Cup playoffs.

"In this league it's not about individual points, it's not about getting goals. It's about getting wins," says Tim. "I think a lot of players would trade their points for getting more wins. And that's how I see it too."

That sounds like a leader talking — something Tim has become on this promising Senators team. And that's exactly what they expected when they drafted him

DID YOU KNOW?

At the 2021 World Junior Hockey Championships, Tim was named the top forward in the tournament. He led the German team to a berth in the quarterfinals, scoring 5 goals and picking up 5 assists in 5 games.

HOCKEY MEMORIES

Many of Tim's early hockey memories have him on roller blades and not skates. "I used to play roller hockey all the time on the street with my dad and some friends from the neighbourhood. The bonds you build and the friendships from playing hockey are so nice."

2023–2024 STATS

GP	G	A	PTS
75	18	52	70

Ottawa Senators' 1st choice, 3rd overall, in 2020 NHL Entry Draft
1st NHL Team, season: Ottawa Senators, 2020–2021
Born: January 15, 2002, in Viersen, Germany
Plays: Center
Shoots: Left
Height: 1.83 m (6'0")
Weight: 89.5 kg (197 lbs.)

PWHL SUPERSTARS

The Professional Women's Hockey League was established in August of 2023, with founding franchises in Toronto, Montreal, Ottawa, Boston, Minneapolis-St. Paul and New York City. Minnesota were the inaugural champions of the PWHL and were awarded the Walter Cup on May 29, 2024. Here are some of the best players in the league:

Natalie Spooner

Marie-Philip Poulin

Kateřina Mrázová

NATALIE SPOONER (F) — TORONTO

Natalie has been a mainstay of Canada's National Women's Team. Last season she led Toronto, and the league, in scoring with 27 points. She's a force in close — in front of the net — something Toronto coach Troy Ryan has stressed to her.

"I challenged her a couple of years ago to tell me where she could be the best in the world," said Ryan. "We identify and she identifies that that's the area where she's her best."

MARIE-PHILIP POULIN (F) — MONTREAL

Marie-Philip Poulin is the only player in women's hockey history to have scored a goal in three Olympic Gold Medal games. Two of those goals were game winners! Last season she was Montreal's leading scorer with 23 points.

"The PWHL is the outcome of years of hard work from key players in the hockey community," says Marie-Philip. "We have achieved a very important milestone, not only for our generation of players but for all of the girls who aspire to play in a professional league one day."

KATEŘINA MRÁZOVÁ (F) — OTTAWA

When the veteran Czech National Team player first took up the game as a young girl in Czechia, she stood out.

"Back home in 1995, girls didn't play hockey. I didn't mind. I immediately fell in love with the sport. Since I was very young when I started playing, I was perfectly at ease with the boys. I think it was the same for them. I was part of the team."

ALINA MÜLLER (F) — BOSTON

Swiss-born Alina Müller had an outstanding college career with the Northeastern Huskies, where she still holds several records, including most career points (254) and game winning goals (28).

"Boston is my second home," said Alina. "After five years as a Husky, I wasn't ready to leave yet. I am super excited to represent Boston alongside some of the best players in the world."

Alina Müller

ALEX CARPENTER (F) — NEW YORK

Alex Carpenter led New York last season with 23 points, and has been a member of the senior U.S. National Women's Team since 2013. Alex's dad, Bobby, played 18 seasons and over 1100 games in the NHL. Alex spent many a night on a backyard rink built by her dad, shooting pucks.

Alex Carpenter

KENDALL COYNE SCHOFIELD (F) — MINNESOTA

Kendall Coyne Schofield has starred for the U.S. National Women's Team at the Women's World Championship and caught the eye of many NHL fans when she participated in the NHL All-Star Weekend Skills Competition in 2019. Her hopes for the league are clear: "For both boys and girls to grow up and say that women can play professional hockey and men can play professional hockey."

Kendall Coyne Schofield

Countdown to the Cup 2024–2025

EASTERN CONFERENCE

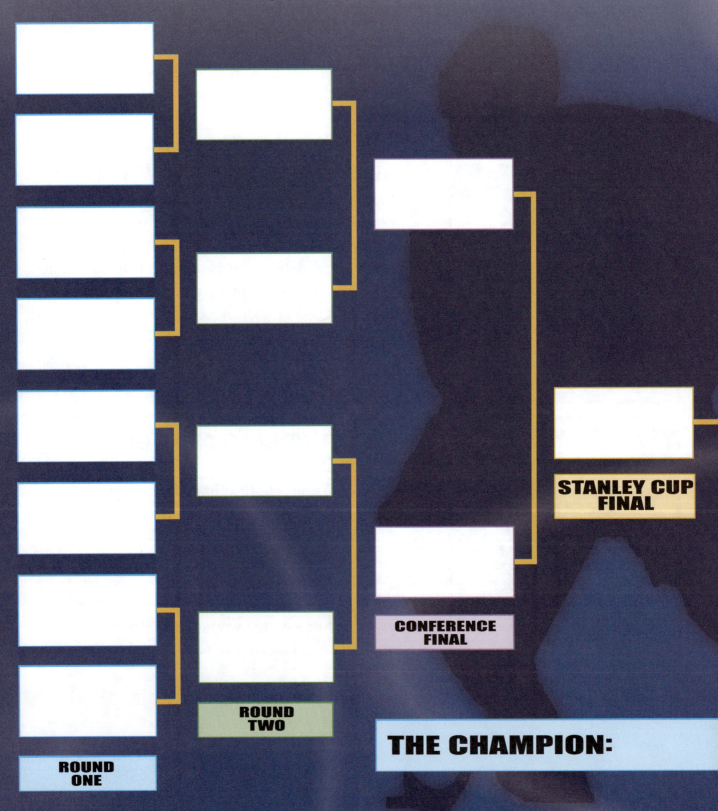

STANLEY CUP FINAL

CONFERENCE FINAL

ROUND TWO

ROUND ONE

THE CHAMPION:

WESTERN CONFERENCE

CONFERENCE FINAL

ROUND TWO

ROUND ONE

NHL AWARDS

Here are some of the major NHL awards for individual players. Fill in your selection for each award and then fill in the name of the actual winner of the trophy.

HART MEMORIAL TROPHY
Awarded to the player judged to be the most valuable to his team. Selected by the Professional Hockey Writers Association.

2024 winner: **Nathan MacKinnon**

Your choice for 2025: _____

The winner: _____

ART ROSS TROPHY
Awarded to the player who leads the league in scoring points at the end of the regular season.

2024 winner: **Nikita Kucherov**

Your choice for 2025: _____

The winner: _____

CALDER MEMORIAL TROPHY
Awarded to the player selected as the most proficient in his first year of competition in the NHL. Selected by the Professional Hockey Writers Association.

2024 winner: **Connor Bedard**

Your choice for 2025: _____

The winner: _____

JAMES NORRIS TROPHY
Awarded to the defense player who demonstrates throughout his season the greatest all-round ability. Selected by the Professional Hockey Writers Association.

2024 winner: **Quinn Hughes**

Your choice for 2025: _____

The winner: _____

VEZINA TROPHY
Awarded to the goalkeeper judged to be the best. Selected by the NHL general managers.

2024 winner: **Connor Hellebuyck**

Your choice for 2025: _____

The winner: _____

TED LINDSAY AWARD
Awarded to the most outstanding player in the NHL as voted by members of the NHL Players' Association.

2024 winner: **Nathan MacKinnon**

Your choice for 2025: _____

The winner: _____

MAURICE RICHARD TROPHY

Awarded to the player who scores the highest number of regular-season goals.

2024 winner: **Auston Matthews**

Your choice for 2025: _____

The winner: _____

FRANK J. SELKE TROPHY

Awarded to the forward who best excels in the defensive aspects of the game. Selected by the Professional Hockey Writers Association.

2024 winner: **Aleksander Barkov**

Your choice for 2025: _____

The winner: _____

WILLIAM M. JENNINGS TROPHY

Awarded to the goalkeeper(s) who played a minimum of 25 games for the team with the fewest goals scored against it.

2024 winners: **Connor Hellebuyck**

Your choice for 2025: _____

The winner: _____

CONN SMYTHE TROPHY

Awarded to the player most valuable to his team in the Stanley Cup playoffs. Selected by the Professional Hockey Writers Association.

2024 winner: **Connor McDavid**

Your choice for 2025: _____

The winner: _____

LADY BYNG MEMORIAL TROPHY

Awarded to the player judged to have exhibited the best sportsmanship combined with a high standard of playing ability. Selected by the Professional Hockey Writers Association.

2024 winner: **Jaccob Slavin**

Your choice for 2025: _____

The winner: _____

BILL MASTERTON MEMORIAL TROPHY

Awarded to the player who best exemplifies the qualities of perseverance, sportsmanship and dedication to hockey. Selected by the Professional Hockey Writers Association.

2024 winner: **Connor Ingram**

Your choice for 2025: _____

The winner: _____

REFEREE SIGNALS

Do you know what is happening when the referee stops play and makes a penalty call? If you don't, then you're missing an important part of the game. The referee can call different penalties that result in anything from playing a man short for two minutes to having a player kicked out of the game.

Here are some of the most common referee signals. Now you'll know what penalties are being called against your team.

Boarding
Checking an opponent into the boards in a violent way.

Cross-checking
Striking an opponent with the stick, while both hands are on the stick and both arms are extended.

Charging
Checking an opponent in a violent way as a result of skating or charging at him.

Elbowing
Checking an opponent with an elbow.

High-sticking
Striking an opponent with the stick, which is held above shoulder height.

Holding
Holding back an opponent
with the hands or arms.

Hooking
Using the blade of the stick
to hold back an opponent.

Icing
Shooting the puck across
the opposing team's goal
line from one's own side
of the rink. Called only
if the opposing player
touches the puck first.

Interference
Holding back an
opponent who does not
have the puck in play.

Kneeing
Using a knee to hold
back an opponent.

Misconduct
A ten-minute penalty — the
longest type called. Usually
for abuse of an official.

Roughing
Shoving or striking an opponent.

REFEREE SIGNALS

Slashing
Using the stick to strike an opponent.

Spearing
Poking an opponent with the blade of the stick.

Slow whistle
The official waits to blow his whistle because of a delayed offside or delayed penalty call. Done while the opposing team has control of the puck.

Tripping
Tripping an opponent with the stick, a hand or a foot.

Unsportsmanlike conduct
Showing poor sportsmanship toward an opponent. For example: biting, pulling hair, etc.

Wash-out
Goal not allowed.